WATCH OUT!

On the Road

Elizabeth Clark

Photographer: Angus Blackburn

Consultants: The Royal Society for the Prevention of Accidents

Artist: Roger Fereday

At Home

Near Water

On My Own

On the Road

Editor: Sarah Doughty
Design concept: Loraine Hayes

First published in 1991 by
Wayland (Publishers) Ltd
61 Western Road, Hove
East Sussex BN3 1JD, England

© Copyright 1991 Wayland (Publishers) Ltd

British Library Cataloguing in Publication Data

Clark, Elizabeth
On the road.
1. Great Britain. Road safety
I. Title II. Series
363.1259

ISBN 0 7502 0052 9

Phototypeset by Dorchester Typesetting Group Ltd

Printed and bound by Casterman S.A., Belgium

Contents

On the road	**4**
Crossing the road	**8**
On your bicycle	**16**
Riding in the car	**22**
Using the bus	**24**
Helping others	**26**
Glossary	**30**
Books to read	**31**
Index	**32**

All the words that appear in
bold are explained in the
glossary on page 30.

WATCH OUT!

On the road

Roads are dangerous places. Our roads are busy and the **traffic** that uses them moves very fast.

Every day people have **accidents** on the roads. To help stop accidents everyone must watch out. We must all think about keeping safe.

People who go on foot are called pedestrians. Pedestrians should walk on the **pavement**, away from the edge of the **kerb**.

Remember, it is very dangerous to play on the pavement or run into the road.

Even on the pavement you have to watch out. The pavement may become dangerous in places where **vehicles** can cross into a driveway.

Derek and his mother make sure the car has pulled into the driveway before they walk across it.

Some roads do not have pavements, so Derek and his sister Tracey walk carefully on the right-hand side of the road.

They can see vehicles coming towards them and can easily be seen by drivers.

When it gets darker, it is a good idea to wear something bright so you can be seen more easily.

Derek and Tracey both wear **reflective strips** on their arms. Derek has a bright yellow bag and Tracey wears a reflective belt.

WATCH OUT!

Crossing the road

When vehicles are moving it is hard to tell how far away they are, and how fast they are going. That is why you must look for the safest way to cross.

Simran and Ryan are using a foot-bridge with Simran's mum. This takes them safely above the road and all the vehicles.

Ryan and George have used the subway to cross the road.

A subway is a tunnel that goes underneath the road, away from all the vehicles.

Outside the school the **school-crossing patrol** helps everyone to cross the road safely.

Other people who will help you cross the road are a police officer or a **traffic warden.**

There are also special crossings for pedestrians.

At the **pelican crossing**, Derek presses the button and waits with his dad. He can see a red person lit up on the signal box on the other side of the road. This tells him that it is not safe to cross.

When the green person lights up it is safe to cross with care. Pedestrians can also hear a bleeping sound. This tells a blind person when it is safe to cross the road.

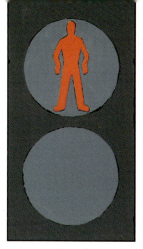  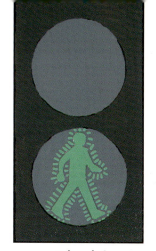

Red person
Do not cross

Steady green person
Cross carefully

Flashing green person
Do not start to cross

This picture shows you when you can cross at a pelican crossing.

These people are using the **zebra crossing**.

They stopped at the kerb and waited for the traffic to stop on both sides of the road.

When they cross they always walk on the black and white stripes painted on the road.

11

Young children should cross the road with a grown-up or an older friend. Talk to this person about road safety.

Always choose a safe place to cross, away from bends in the road and parked cars. Make sure you can see traffic clearly both ways. When you cross the road always use the Green Cross Code:

1. First, find a safe place to cross, then stop.

2. Stand on the pavement near the kerb.

3. Look all round for traffic and listen.

4. If traffic is coming, let it pass. Look all round again.

5. When there is no traffic near, walk straight across.

6. Keep looking and listening while you cross.

A **traffic island** is a safe place in the middle of the road. This helps you to cross one half of the road at a time.

Simran and Ryan have crossed to the island. They used the Green Cross Code. Now they are looking and listening to see if the road is clear before crossing safely.

Can you say where the safe places to cross are in this picture? Can you see any places where it would be unsafe to try and cross?

Answers on page 32

15

WATCH OUT!

On your bicycle

Khai has asked his dad to check that his bicycle is the right size for him.

He makes sure that Khai can reach the handlebars and brakes easily without leaning forward, and that he can touch the ground with his toes.

Khai's dad thinks that the saddle of his bicycle is too low and not safe.

He adjusts it so that it is higher.

Do you know how to check your bicycle to keep it safe? You and a grown-up should often check the tyres, the lights and brakes.

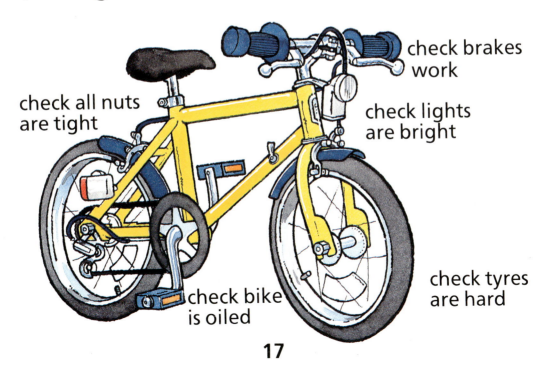

Scott's dad makes sure that the brakes on Scott's bike are safe.

Lesley-Ann and Scott always put on their helmets before they set off on their bicycles.

Lesley-Ann is only six so she rides her bicycle in the park.

She never rides on the pavement or on the road because she could have an accident.

Her mum, dad or older brother always come with her when she is riding.

Always sit on the saddle to ride. Pedal with the balls of your feet. Keep your hands on the grips near the brake levers.

Gordon has gone cycling with his parents on a quiet road.

They cycle on the left of the road, near the kerb. They do not cycle side by side as this could cause an accident.

When the family want to turn left, they each make a signal with their left arm.

They wait at the road junction until the road is clear. Then they cycle carefully left.

Gordon and his parents need to cross the busy road with their bicycles.

To be safe, they wait on the kerb until there is no traffic coming, then walk their bicycles across the road.

WATCH OUT!

Riding in the car

Derek and Tracey always sit in the back seat of the car.

They wear seat belts to keep them safe. Derek sits on a **booster seat** which lifts him up higher in the seat.

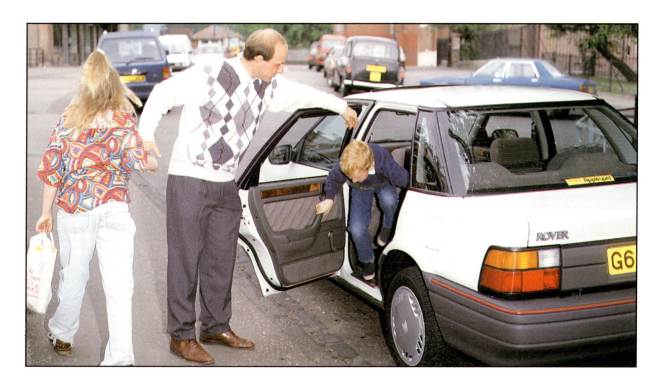

When Derek and Tracey get in or out of the car, they always use the door near the pavement or path. Can you say why this is safer?

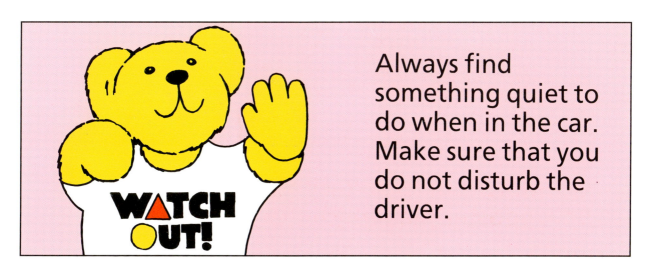

Always find something quiet to do when in the car. Make sure that you do not disturb the driver.

WATCH OUT!

Using the bus

Ryan and George stand well back at the bus stop and do not play games as this could cause an accident.

They wait for other people to get off the bus before they get on.

This stops anyone being injured in the doorway.

When Ryan and George get off the bus, they let it move away before trying to cross the road.

This is so they can see what other vehicles are on the road. Drivers can also see them.

25

WATCH OUT!
Helping others

The people in the picture are making life easier and safer for others by walking carefully on the pavement and giving other people plenty of room. In what other ways are they being helpful?

Eleie is helping other people by throwing away her litter safely.

Can you think of ways in which litter could cause an accident?

Eleie is talking to a disabled friend. People in wheelchairs need plenty of room when they are using the pavement or crossing the road.

Remember, disabled people may not be able to move to one side as easily as you can.

Glossary

Accident An event that happens by mistake.

Booster seat A raised safety seat for a child.

Kerb The edge of the pavement.

Pavement A raised area at the side of the road, where it is safe to walk.

Pelican crossing A crossing place where you press a button to work a signal which tells the traffic to stop, and you to cross.

Reflective strip A strip made of a material which reflects the light of a car headlamp and shows the driver where you are.

School-crossing patrol (lollipop person) A person who wears a white coat and carries a large round sign on a pole. This tells the traffic to stop so children can cross the road safely.

Traffic All the vehicles which use the road.

Traffic island A raised area in the middle of the road.

Traffic warden A person who is in charge of watching over road traffic.

Vehicle Any form of transport with wheels.

Zebra crossing A crossing with black and white stripes painted on the road.

Books to read

Crossing Roads by Althea (Dinosaur Publications, 1988)

Let's Go Across the Road by Rachel Wise (Franklin Watts, 1980)

On the Road by Pete Sanders (Franklin Watts, 1989)

Safety On the Road by Dorothy Baldwin and Claire Lister (Wayland, 1986)

Notes for parents and teachers

Children are good imitators. If they see you using good road habits, they will learn by example.

Before the age of seven, children cannot estimate the speed of traffic accurately or judge whether they have enough time to cross a road safely. A child should always be accompanied by a grown-up, who should hold his or her hand when going out into the road.

Use safe places to cross the road where possible such as pedestrian crossings, foot-bridges or subways. You can involve your child from an early age in ideas about road safety by talking through each situation. Later on, encourage your child to show you that he or she can recognize safe places to cross

and that he or she remembers to STOP, LOOK and LISTEN.

Make sure your child's bicycle is suitable for his or her size and age. Ensure the bicycle's tyres, brakes and steering are checked regularly. Children under nine should always ride in a safe place such as a park or garden, not on the road or pavement. They should always be accompanied by a grown-up or an older, responsible brother or sister. If you take your child cycling with you on the road, choose a quiet road and cycle behind his or her bicycle.

Children can take the National Cycling Proficiency Test at nine years old. Ask at school about 'Cycleway', an extended version of the course, or contact the local road safety officer for details.

When travelling in the car, the safest place for any child is in the rear seat, wearing a properly designed restraint device. This may be a special car seat or booster cushion, and a seat belt. If seat belts are installed in the back of the car, it is the driver's legal responsibility for children under 14 to use them.

If you would like your child to join the Tufty Club to learn more about safety, write to RoSPA at:
Safety Education Department
Cannon House
The Priory Queensway
Birmingham, B4 6BS.

If you would like your child to join the National Bike Club and learn more about safe and enjoyable cycling write to the National Bike Club at the RoSPA address.

Index

Bicycle 16, 17, 18, 19, 20, 21
Bus 24, 25

Car 22, 23
Cycling 19, 20, 21

Disabled people 10, 27
Driveway 6

Foot-bridge 8

Green Cross Code 12, 13, 14

Hand signals 21
Helping people 26, 27

Pedestrians 5, 9, 10
Pelican crossing 10, 11

Reflective gear 7

School-crossing patrol 9
Seat belts 22
Subway 9

Traffic island 14
Traffic warden 9

Vehicles 6, 7, 8, 9, 25

Zebra crossing 11

Answers to page 15
Safer places to cross are on the foot-bridge, at a zebra crossing or a pelican crossing, and on a quiet road where you can see traffic coming clearly. Dangerous places to cross are at a roundabout, on a busy road, near junctions and bends in the road, near a hump-back bridge which blocks the view, near a parked bus, car and ice-cream van.

Answers to pages 28-29
There are many people who are not thinking about safety. They include: car drivers not stopping at red traffic lights, cars on the pavement obstructing pedestrians, a group chatting in the road near a parked van, a child playing ball on the pavement, children on skateboards and roller skates, a parent not supervising a toddler, pet owners not looking after their animals, and a cyclist riding badly.